MORE SECRET LIVES OF TEACHERS

Brian Moses lives in Sussex with his wife and two daughters. Before becoming a full-time writer, he worked as a teacher and can verify that everything in this book is true (well almost!).

Lucy Maddison lives in Balham, London, with Brian the boyfriend, Patrick the lodger and Bubbles the cat. She'd make a hopeless teacher as she can't even teach Bubbles to use the cat flap.

Also available from Macmillan

THE SECRET LIVES OF TEACHERS
Revealing Rhymes chosen by Brian Moses

ALIENS STOLE MY UNDERPANTS
and other Intergalactic Poems
chosen by Brian Moses

PARENT-FREE ZONE
Poems about Parents and other Problems
chosen by Brian Moses

'ERE WE GO!
Football Poems chosen by David Orme

YOU'LL NEVER WALK ALONE
More Football Poems chosen by David Orme

WE WAS ROBBED
Yet More Football Poems chosen by David Orme

NOTHING TASTES QUITE LIKE A GERBIL
and other Vile Verses chosen by David Orme

SNOGGERS
Slap 'n' Tickle Poems chosen by David Orme

CUSTARD PIE
Poems that are Jokes that are Poems
chosen by Pie Corbett

TONGUE TWISTERS AND TONSIL TWIZZLERS
Poems chosen by Paul Cookson

MORE SECRET LIVES OF TEACHERS

More Revealing Rhymes

CHOSEN BY
BRIAN MOSES

ILLUSTRATED BY
LUCY MADDISON

MACMILLAN CHILDREN'S BOOKS

For all those children – and some teachers –
who said good things about the first book . . .
Here we go again!

First published 1997 by
Macmillan Children's Books
a division of Macmillan Publishers Ltd
25 Eccleston Place, London SW1W 9NF
and Basingstoke

Associated companies throughout the world

ISBN 0 330 34994 5

7 9 8

A CIP catalogue record for this book is available from the British Library.

Printed by Mackays of Chatham PLC, Chatham, Kent.

'Romance' by Brian Moses first appeared in *Croc City*
published by the Victoria Press 1993.

CONTENTS

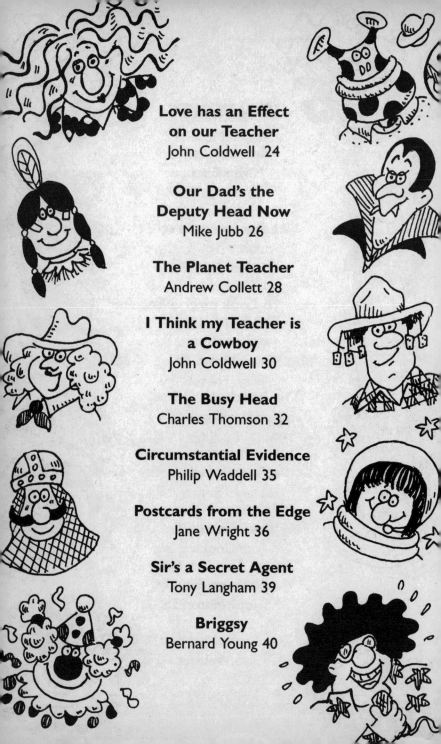

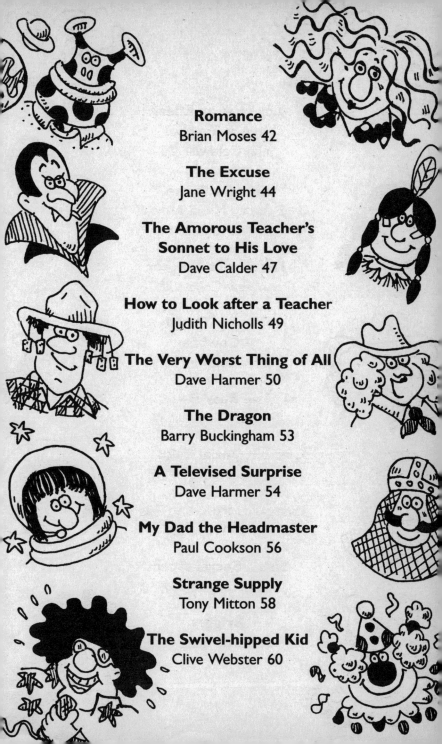

Secret Love

Chalked on a wall in the playground,
These words inside a heart:
'David loves Susan forever,
And we shall never part.'

David loves Susan
forever
and we shall
never part

But nobody knew, and nobody guessed,
The secret behind what it said:
That Dave was the History teacher,
And Sue was the Deputy Head.

Mike Jubb

Our Hippy Teacher

Miss Thomson's vague and dreamy
and given half a chance,
   will meditate through lessons
      and end up in a trance.

         We think she's been a hippy
            as she strongly favours beads.
            Her clothes are psychedelic
            and she makes baskets out of reeds.

      And if you gaze too closely
         in her vague and dreamy eyes
         you discover to your cost
            she has the power to hypnotize.

         'You will obey,' she murmurs.
         'You will study till you drop
            and not until I clap
            are you allowed to stop.'

         And then she puts her feet up
            with a mild, contented smirk
      and dreams away till hometime
      while we do all the work.

   Marian Swinger

Escape Route

When our teacher came to school today
he looked bright and happy, not old and grey,
not the usual bear whose head was sore,
and we hadn't seen him like this before.
He parked his car in our headteacher's space,
you should have seen the look on her face
as she swept like a hurricane into our room,
and it brightened up our Monday gloom.
But instead of looking a picture of worry
or smiling nervously and saying sorry
he'd go out and shift it straightaway,
our teacher told her that from today
she could stay and teach his class,
and the look on her face was like frosted glass.
He ripped up test papers in front of her eyes,
then jumped up and down, and to our surprise
planted a slobbery kiss on her cheek
and just for a moment she couldn't speak
till he told us how on Saturday night
his lottery numbers had all been right.
Then a noise from outside made us all look round
as a helicopter landed in our school grounds,
and our teacher said, 'It's my taxi at last,
this school, all of you, are now in my past.'
Then while we watched, the big blades whirred
and he left for the sky as free as a bird.

And his car is still parked in our headteacher's space.
You should have seen the look on her face!

Brian Moses

The I-Spy Book of Teachers

One point if you catch your teacher yawning,
double that to two if later on you find him snoring,
Three points if you hear your teacher singing

and four if it's a pop song not a hymn.
A generous five points if you ever see him jogging
and six if you should chance upon him snogging.

Seven if you ever find him on his knees and praying
for relief from noisy boys who trouble him.
Eight if you should catch him in the betting shop,

nine if you see him dancing on *Top of the Pops*,
And ten if you hear him say what a lovely class he's got
for then you'll know there's something wrong with him.

Brian Moses

The Teacher's Curse

'Hateful pupils,' muttered Mrs Pye.
'Beastly, cheeky, lazy little brats.
Stand up that child who hit me in the eye.
Arise, foul missile thrower, like a man.'

Headmaster Jones popped in and shook his head.
'Disgraceful! Mrs Pye, control your class.'
He slammed the door and Mrs Pye blushed red.
'Revenge,' she muttered, raising high her arms.

The room grew dark, the pupils pale with fright
as Mrs Pye, her eyes a ghastly green,
cried, 'I, Tallora, Mistress of the Night,
call down upon your heads this awful curse.'

The children sat transfixed, with bated breath.
Tallora chanted, 'Teachers you shall be.
A fitting curse, a fate far worse than death.
And now, farewell sweet pupils, I depart.'

And, gliding to the door, Tallora went.
And pupils tittered, but it all came true.
Some now teach in Essex, some in Kent
and some of them could well be teaching you!

Marian Swinger

Hands

Last Saturday, shopping with my mum down town,
I caught a glimpse of Mrs Brown.
She must be 50 if she's a day.
Her face is wrinkled
And she's gone quite grey.
She's very old fashioned,
Wears blacks and blues,
Thick, thick stockings
And granny-type shoes.
But imagine, if you can,
My huge surprise.
I hardly could believe my eyes.
There she was, in the Saturday street,
Just as usual, greyly neat,
But walking along arm in arm
And holding the hand
Of a rock star from my favourite band.

And then I tell you
(I nearly missed it)
He took her hand
And gently kissed it!

And then my mum whispered
In a voice that just carried,
'But didn't you know
Those two are married?
Mrs Brown's been married to him for years.'

I hardly could believe my ears.
Who would have thought
Rock stars could ever have wives –
Or that teachers could ever
Have such secret lives?

John Kitching

Whispers of Love

Janis Priestley

What Teacher did on her Holidays

She flew a plane and looped the loop
She dropped her glasses in the soup
She knitted a jumper without arms
She set off Sainsbury's fire alarms
She played for Spurs and scored a goal
She made rock cakes and a sausage roll
She went to the zoo and was chased by a bear
She lost her marbles down the back of a chair
She went for a swim and was swept out to sea
She was rescued by a chimpanzee
She beat Steve Davis and potted the black
Good morning teacher
We're glad you're back.

Roger Stevens

Love has an Effect on our Teacher

When our teacher fell in love with a doctor
She was ill every day of the week
When she fell in love with a plumber
Her radiator sprang a leak
When she fell in love with a dustman
She put her bin out every day
When she fell in love with a farmer
She spent the weekends baling hay
When she fell for a librarian
She was always borrowing books
When she fell in love with a policeman
She went chasing after crooks.

But when another teacher
Took our teacher's attention
They got married straight away
And kept each other in detention.

John Coldwell

Our Dad's the Deputy Head Now

Our dad's the Deputy Head now;
The kids all think he's hateful.
At least we've moved to a different school,
For which we are 'truly grateful'.
They say he's more bossy than ever,
Now that he's got more clout;
He stalks along the corridors
And puts some stick about.

'What do you think *you're* doing?
Wipe that smile off your face;
Who do you think you're talking to?
You're an absolute disgrace!'

At home, Dad's the same as ever.
The kids would have a laugh
If they saw him in Mum's pink shower cap
When he's singing in the bath.
At night, he goes out in the garden
For what he calls 'self-defence';
He picks up slugs and throws them
Over next door's garden fence.
When Mum told him off for it,
He snapped, 'I beg your pardon,
I'm paying them back for what their cat
Keeps doing in my garden.'

At school, our dad is the Deputy Head
He stands for Law and Order.
At home, he doesn't know yet:
We've been using his camcorder!

Mike Jubb

The Planet Teacher

On a planet not far from here,
a planet painted green,
you can hear the quiet hum
of the teacher-making machine.

28

For teachers are not born,
they're not like you or me.
No, teachers are made from dust
then given away for free.

They're packed in big brown boxes
with a coffee cup at the back,
two packets of smart red pens
and a National Curriculum pack.

They come with full instructions
and trousers that never fit,
and half a dozen odd socks
from a special odd-sock kit.

And finally they're wrapped
in coloured bits of straw,
before being dropped, on demand,
through someone's staffroom door.

Andrew Collett

I Think my Teacher is a Cowboy

It's not just
That she rides to school on a horse
And carries a Colt 45 in her handbag.

It's not just
the way she walks;
hands hanging over her hips.

It's not just
the way she dresses;
stetson hat and spurs on her boots.

It's not just the way she talks;
calling the playground the corral,
   the Head's room the Sheriff's office,
   the school canteen the chuck wagon,
   the school bus the stage coach,
   the bike sheds the livery stable.

What gives her away
Is when the hometime pips go.
She slaps her thigh
And cries
'Yee ha!'

John Coldwell

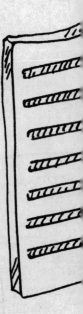

The Busy Head

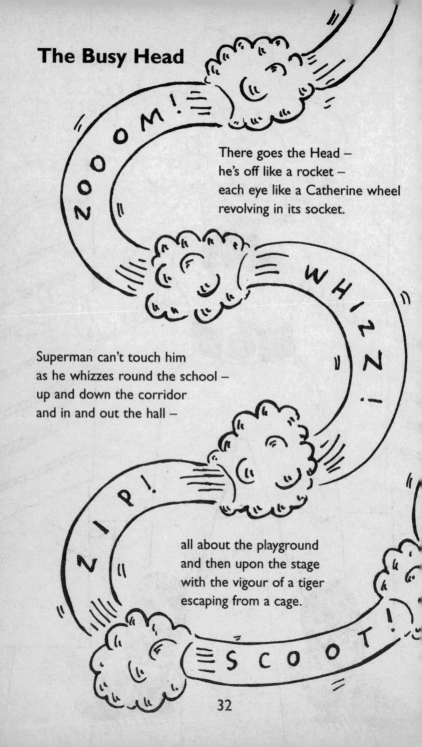

There goes the Head –
he's off like a rocket –
each eye like a Catherine wheel
revolving in its socket.

Superman can't touch him
as he whizzes round the school –
up and down the corridor
and in and out the hall –

all about the playground
and then upon the stage
with the vigour of a tiger
escaping from a cage.

He breaks the speed of sound
with a supersonic blast
and there's just a flash of light
to say the Head's gone past.

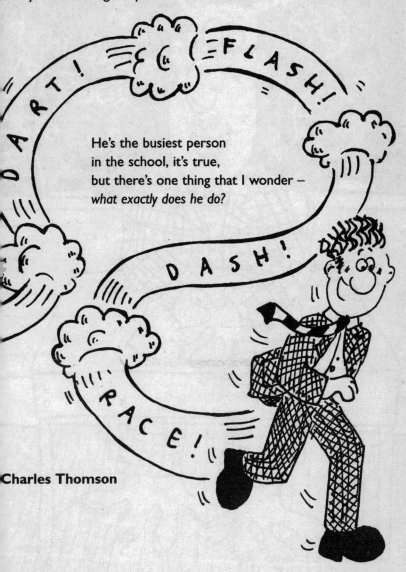

He's the busiest person
in the school, it's true,
but there's one thing that I wonder —
what exactly does he do?

Charles Thomson

Circumstantial Evidence

Mr Tramain, our science teacher, is a space alien.
For a start he's much too old to be human —
'*Two hundred*!' he irritably let slip when I asked.

Also he's telepathic — when he says
'*I know what you're up to, boy!*'
He's always right.

Sometimes when he's teaching he forgets to speak our tongue,
Just drones on in some scientific language
So that we've no idea what he's on about.

Once he told us he was interested in astronomy —
Said he had a telescope at home to gaze at the stars,
Just suffers from homesickness I bet!

His wife's called Zara, or some such, and their kid is Zak —
Alien names if ever I've heard them —
And he's admitted they come from somewhere *far away*.

In last year's pantomime
He appeared as the not-very-jolly green giant —
I bet he just *removed* his make-up for that part.

But what absolutely convinces me
(I must warn our headmaster Mr Greenman-Little)
Is I've just rearranged the letters in Tramain!

Philip Waddell

Postcard from the Edge

Dear Class_____(*fill in year*)

I'm having ☐ a wonderful time ☐ sweet dreams of you
☐ a nervous breakdown.

We arrived after sixteen ☐ hours ☐ days ☐ Hell's Angels
helped us fix our flat tyre.

Still, the hotel is ☐ atop a huge cliff ☐ sliding over the cliff
☐ not built yet

and the views over ☐ the sea ☐ the bins ☐ Tesco's car park
are staggering.

I'd like to ☐ take in the sea air ☐ teach the world to sing
☐ strangle every one of you personally

but the doctor says ☐ I should take it easy ☐ I'm a raving loony
☐ I need help.

You mustn't think ☐ I don't miss you ☐ I like you
☐ because it hurts your head.

But I must admit taking this holiday is exactly
☐ what I needed ☐ what you needed ☐ what the rest of the
staff needed.

I know that little chemistry experiment was
☐ an accident ☐ an act of genius ☐ an act of sabotage

and that you didn't mean ☐ for it to happen ☐ to blow up the
school ☐ to set my cardigan on fire.

Auntie June ☐ is looking after me very well ☐ is sick of the sight
of me ☐ has fallen in love with one of the Hell's Angels
and says I should be up and about by ☐ next week ☐ next
Christmas ☐ the time she counts to three
otherwise ☐ she'll have to get the doctor back ☐ she'll shout
for Uncle Alfie ☐ there'll be trouble.
See you ☐ soon I hope ☐ not if I see you first ☐ in court.
Your ☐ loving ☐ demented ☐ redundant teacher,
_____(sign here).

Jane Wright

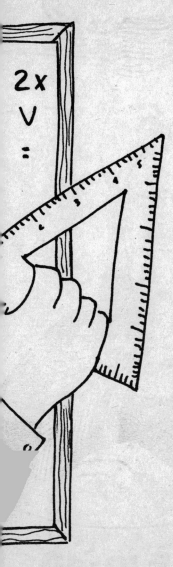

Sir's a Secret Agent

Sir's a secret agent
He's licensed to thrill
At Double-Oh Sevening
He's got bags of skill.

He's tall, dark and handsome
With a muscular frame
Teaching's his profession
But Danger's his game!

He's cool and he's calm
When he makes a decision
He's a pilot, sky-diver
And can teach long-division.

No mission's too big
No mission's too small
School-kids, mad scientists
He takes care of them all.

He sorts out the villains
The spies and the crooks
Then comes back to school
And marks all our books!

Tony Langham

Briggsy

It's her birthday.
She doesn't want anyone to know.
She's not intending to celebrate
hitting the big 4 0.

Yes, today Mrs Briggs is forty.
You can't tell. It doesn't show.
(And even if you think it does
don't you dare say so.)

Because TODAY MRS BRIGGS IS FORTY
and she doesn't want anyone to know.

Although,
when someone in class has a birthday
she announces it
and makes a big fuss

so

we'd like to make a big fuss of Mrs Briggs.
We've written a poem for her.
(We're planning to perform it in assembly.)

It goes like this:

Mrs Briggs you're forty
That's quite an age to reach

Mrs Briggs you're forty
Long may you teach

Mrs Briggs you're forty
You don't want a fuss

Mrs Briggs you're forty
Your secret's safe with us

CONGRATULATIONS MRS BRIGGS ON TURNING 40

It's called *Mrs Briggs You're Forty*
and we hope she likes it.

Bernard Young

41

Romance

I know there's something going on
between Mr Phipps and Miss White.
I've seen them in the car park,
how they linger when they say goodnight.

I caught them once in the TV room
with all of the blinds drawn down.
He said that he'd lost his glasses,
I bet they were fooling around.

When she wafts into our classroom
and catches him by surprise,
nothing is too much trouble,
there's a faraway look in his eyes.

Quite what she sees in him,
none of us really knows:
She's quite fashion conscious,
he wears some terrible clothes.

We think he sends her notes:
Please tick if you really love me,
and if she's slow to reply
We've seen him get awfully angry.

But when they're lovey-dovey,
He's just like a little boy,
cracking jokes and smiling again,
filling our class with his joy.

Brian Moses

The Excuse

She walked in nervously, biting her lip;
Trembling slightly, she could not meet their gaze.
'WELL?' shouted the class together –
Startled, the teacher made for the desk where
Behind the relative security of four wooden legs and
a jar of fading daisies
She felt an explanation coming on.
'WHERE'S OUR HOMEWORK?' yelled the class.
'Erm, well,' said the teacher, 'I haven't got it with me.'
'A LIKELY STORY,' sneered the class.
'YOU HAVEN'T DONE IT, HAVE YOU?' chorused the class.
'YOU HAVEN'T EVEN BOTHERED TO MARK OUR
    HOMEWORK!' they cried.
Inside her head she scrabbled desperately for something
    believable,
Sweat trickling down her temple and inside her palms.
'I dropped it getting off the bus. It landed
in a puddle then a
Huge gang of teachers took it off me and said
I wouldn't be let into the Staffroom Coffee-Tea Rotation
    Posse if I did it.
"Marking homework is for wimps," they said,' she said sadly,
a big round tear rolling slowly down her cheek.
'OH,' said the class, shifting uncomfortably,
'WELL, JUST MAKE SURE YOU HAVE IT FOR TOMORROW.
THERE, THERE. NO NEED TO CRY.'
'Thank you, class,' sniffed the teacher, brightening a little,
'It won't happen again, I promise.'

Jane Wright

The Amorous Teacher's Sonnet to His Love

Each morning I teach in a daze until
the bell that lets me hurry down and queue
with pounding heart to wait for you to fill
my eyes with beauty and my plate with stew.
Dear dinner lady, apple of my eye,
I long to shout *I love you* through the noise
and take your hand across the shepherd's pie
despite the squealing girls or snickering boys.
O let us flee together and start up
a little café somewhere in the Lakes
and serve day trippers tea in china cups
and buttered scones on pretty patterned plates.

Alas for dreams so rudely bust in two –
some clumsy child's spilt custard on my shoe.

Dave Calder

MY CUSTARD!

How to Look After a Teacher

Don't cross him on Monday morning
before he's quite awake;
if you want a peaceful classroom
keep out of his way at break.
(If you must thump Jamie,
do it round the corner.)

Always offer a sweet or crisp –
especially when eating in class;
admire his chronic taste in clothes
if you don't want extra maths.
(Perhaps he really likes
flared jeans with orange socks.)

Don't ask if he's wearing a wig today –
you'll only make him sore.
When he starts to say 'When I was at school . . .'
don't add, 'In the Boer War!'
(He can't really help being
an old man of thirty.)

Judith Nicholls

groovy!

Please note

SPS

YUM!

I'm only 30!

The Very Worst Thing of All

If you see
your mum and dad holding hands
it's embarrassing.

If you catch them
plant even the slightest peck on the cheek
it's dreadful.

If your mum
kisses you when you get out of the car
in front of everyone at school
it's awful.

If Darren the Slob and Dean the Blob
chase you around the yard
and try to kiss you
it's so revolting
you are sick for days.

But if you go to the pictures
with your best friend Julie
and just as the lights go down
as you begin to guzzle popcorn
you see Mr Evans, your class teacher,
slip a long and snaky arm
round the shoulders of Miss Carter,
who is of course your other teacher,
it really is the worst thing in the world.

It makes you go all red and burning
it makes you fizz and gasp
it makes your toenails tingle
it makes your stomach tremble
and you and Julie giggle
very loudly.

Of course
it's even worse for them
when they turn round
and see you.

David Harmer

HEAD TEACHER

The Dragon

Why do they call her 'The Dragon',
our fiery head teacher, Miss Quail?
  She's really quite nice,
  though she's told me off twice
when I've swung on a dangerous rail.

She can't help her big flaring nostrils —
great holes at the end of her snout.
  I'm sure it's a joke —
  must be cigarette smoke
that we sometimes see billowing out.

They say that the walls in her study
have claw marks right up to the ceiling.
  But some little twits
  drive her out of her wits,
so she must get a desperate feeling.

But why do they call her 'The Dragon'?
It seems so unfair to Miss Quail.
  She's normal to me —
  well, from what I can see
of her arms and her legs . . . and her tail!

Barry Buckingham

A Televised Surprise

Imagine our delight
Consternation and surprise
Our teacher on *Come Dancing*
Right before our eyes.

She wore a dress of sequins
That glittered like a flight
Of silent, silver snowflakes
On a winter's night.

She really looked fantastic
No one could ignore
The magic of her dancing
Across the ballroom floor.

Her partner, tall and smart,
Only saw him from the back,
His hair was slicked down short
His suit and shoes were black.

He whirled and twirled her round
As the music got much faster
And then faced the camera
It was our Headmaster!

They seemed to dance for ever
Until it wasn't fun
And the competition stopped
The pair of them had won.

David Harmer

My Dad the Headmaster

My dad the Headmaster knows every single rule
and when he is at home he thinks that he's at school.
He rings the bell each morning and I'd better not be late
so I'm washed and down for breakfast at exactly ten to eight.

He stands and takes the register, checks my shirt and tie,
then he says 'Good Morning' and I have to reply
'Good–Mor–ning–Fa–ther' in that monotone drone
and hear his assembly in my very own home.

He has a list of rules that are pasted on each door:
No Spitting. No Chewing. No Litter On The Floor.
No Music. No Jewellery. No Make-Up. No Telly.
No Making Rude Noises Especially If They're Smelly.

No Videos. No Football. No Coloured Socks Or Laces.
No Trainers. No Jeans. No Smiling Faces.
No Sticking Bubble Gum In Your Sister's Hair.
No Wiping Bogies Down The Side Of The Chair.

He has a list of sayings for all types of occasion
and a set of phrases for every situation:
'Don't run down the stairs. Speak when spoken to.
Put your hand up first if you want to use the loo.

'I don't mind how long I wait. Listen when I'm speaking.
No one leaves the table until we've finished eating.
Don't interrupt and don't answer back.
Don't do this and don't do that.'

Yes, my dad the Headmaster knows every single rule
and when he is at home he thinks that he's at school.
But I am not the only one who does what he is told.
Dad never complains if his dinner is cold.

He's ever so polite when mother is around
and mumbles 'Yes my dear' while looking at the ground.
Her foghorn commands, they really drive him crazy.
Dad's scared stiff of Mum . . . she's a dinner lady!

Paul Cookson

Strange Supply

The work was out and ready.
The room was spick and span.
We all trooped in and took our seats
and the register began.

Our names were called in order.
All of us answered, 'Here!'
Uneasily we waited
for a teacher to appear.

But no one paced the classroom,
or none that we could see.
Only a voice rapped, 'Silence!
Now listen well to me.

'Ms Jones has leave of absence.
I shall not tell you why.
All you need know is simply this:
I am today's Supply.

'You need not seek to see me.
Be sure that I am here,
hovering at your elbow
or hissing in your ear.'

Throughout the day an awful hush
hung on our fearful class.
Our timid pencils crept along
as we prayed for time to pass.

Nobody made a murmur.
Nobody said a thing.
But all of us breathed a sigh when the final
bell began to ring.

So when next day the rumour spread,
'She's back! Ms Jones is here . . . !'
as she stepped through the door,
    the whole of class four
gave one almighty cheer.

Tony Mitton

The Swivel-hipped Kid

Our Music teacher was right old-fashioned –
His name was Mr Sidney.
He went on and on about classical stuff
So we called him 'Sidney Stravinsky'.

'Classical this' and 'classical that',
He rubbished anything pop.
He said that Tchaikovsky and Mozart and such
Was better than soul, rap or rock.

And yet Sid Stravinsky, old-fashioned and quiet
With his minim and crotchet and quaver,
And Schubert and Brahms and a fella called Grieg
Was really a right little raver.

I found out his secret merely by chance
At a club on our caravan site –
They have different things on throughout the week
And Thursday was 'New Talent Nite'.

We'd gone there and found ourselves seats near the front
And the show started off with a swing –
Two or three people just having a laugh
And trying their hardest to sing.

And then came the bombshell; the compere announced,
'And now folks, we've got Swinging Sid.
So let's hear it now, let's give a big hand
For Sid, the Swivel-hipped Kid.'

And old Sid Stravinsky was there in the flesh
With wig and electric guitar,
Shouting and yelling and jumping around
Like an ageing demented pop star.

Old Mr Sidney, who rubbished pop music,
Who was really old-fashioned and quiet,
Was there, like a madman, frantic on stage,
Screaming and starting a riot.

I couldn't believe it, honest I couldn't,
It was just as though I was dreaming –
My music teacher up there on the stage,
Gyrating and yelling and screaming.

And not only that, he came out the winner,
Through to the final no less,
Gyrating and yelling and screaming and such,
Honest, I'd never have guessed.

But I'll give the 'Kid' a nasty surprise,
At the final down there in September –
I'll get up a coachload of kids from our school
For a night he's going to remember.

He'll never again rubbish rap, rock or soul,
The old hypocrite wouldn't dare –.
He knows that we'd all just cry out in one voice,
'Hey Swivel-hipped Kid, WE WERE THERE!!!'

Clive Webster

A selected list of poetry books available from Macmillan

The prices shown below are correct at the time of going to press. However, Macmillan Publishers reserve the right to show new retail prices on covers which may differ from those previously advertised.

The Secret Lives of Teachers 0 330 34265 7
Revealing rhymes, chosen by Brian Moses £3.50

Parent-Free Zone 0 330 34554 0
Poems about parents, chosen by Brian Moses £2.99

You'll Never Walk Alone 0 330 33787 4
More football poems, chosen by David Orme £2.99

We Was Robbed 0 330 35005 6
Yet more football poems, chosen by David Orme £2.99

Nothing Tastes Quite Like a Gerbil 0 330 34632 6
And other vile verses, chosen by David Orme £2.99

Custard Pie 0 330 33992 3
Poems that are jokes, chosen by Pie Corbett £3.50

Tongue Twisters and Tonsil Twizzlers 0 330 34941 4
Poems chosen by Paul Cookson £2.99

All Macmillan titles can be ordered at your local bookshop or are available by post from:

Book Service by Post
PO Box 29, Douglas, Isle of Man IM99 1BQ

Credit cards accepted. For details:
Telephone: 01624 675137
Fax: 01624 670923
E-mail: bookshop@enterprise.net

Free postage and packing in the UK.
Overseas customers: add £1 per book (paperback) and £3 per book (hardback).